Practical College English

실용대학영어

김경태 이근홍 임정현 Catherine Lynn Carriero

정독
DEEP READING

머리말

현대사회는 세계화의 흐름 속에서 급변하고 있으며 글로벌은 이미 우리에게 친숙한 상황으로 깊숙하게 다가와 있다. 이미 오랜 시간 글로벌시대를 살아가는 우리에게 외국어의 활용은 필수적인 요소로 자리잡고 있으며 대표적인 글로벌언어로서 영어의 중요성은 말하지 않아도 일상생활에 보편화가 되어 있다.

이에 정규 교육과정에서 영어를 학습하고 대학에 진학을 하고 있지만 현실은 외국어 언어체계에 대한 이해력이 많이 부족한 나머지 영어의 두려움 등으로 포기하는 학생들이 많은 현실이다. 영어에 대한 두려움은 글로벌시대의 의사소통능력을 저하시키고 나아가 원활한 대인관계를 형성할 수 없는 상황에 놓이게 되며, 다양한 직장에서의 업무능력에도 그 영향이 끼치게 된다.

이러한 상황에 있어 우리에게 필요한 영어지식과 학습능력이 무엇이며 글로벌시대에 필요한 어학능력을 기르기 위한 필수적인 요소를 체계적으로 구성하여 학생들의 이해력과 역량 함양을 고취시키고자 학습자의 학습환경과 요구를 파악하여, 보다 현실적이고 발전적이며 실용적인 교재가 필요하다고 판단되어 본 교재를 집필하였다.

본 교재는 모두 11개의 단원으로 구성하였으며 마지막을 제외한 모든 단원들은 dialogue와 필요에 따른 article을 제공한다. 각 단원별 dialogue와 article을 이해하는데 필요한 어휘와 숙어 등을 정리하고 구문의 정확한 이해를 위한 설명과, 일상이나 여행지 등에서 사용할 수 있는 생활영어표현 등을 제시하여 기본적인 생활영어의 부분을 가미하였다.

또한 다양한 영어 표현들을 읽고 분석하는 것에서 그치지 않고 짝 활동을 통해 핵심 표현을 연습하고 자연스럽게 발화할 수 있도록 보다 실용성 있고 생동감 있는 수업이 이루어지도록 구성하였으며, 교재의 마지막 특별 단원에서는 메타언어(Meta Language)의 기본 의미와 문장의 구조 설명을 제공하여 교재 내용의 이해를 돕도록 하였다.

본 교재를 통해 영어에 대한 두려움을 버리고 기초영어지식과 실용회화를 익히면서 학생들의 역량 함양에 도움을 주고 외국인과의 대인관계에 자심감과 직장에서의 업무수행에 적극적으로 활용할 수 있도록 도움이 되기를 희망한다.

2021년 12월

저자 씀

차 례

UNIT

01

Greetings and Introductions

WARM-UP

A It's nice to meet you.

B Nice to meet you, too.

GUESS

- What do you see in the picture?
- What are they doing?

DIALOGUE

Marissa	Hey, Katie! Come here, I want to introduce you to my friend Zac.
Katie	Hi Zac, it's nice to meet you.
Zac	Same!
Marissa	Zac and I have been friends since elementary school.
Katie	Oh, really?
Zac	Yeah, we met in Kindergarten actually.
Katie	Wow! You've really known each other for a long time!
Zac	How did you and Marissa meet?
Katie	We actually met in Middle School.
Marissa	Yes! In fact, I've known you both for such a long time, I really should have introduced you earlier.
Zac	I can't believe we never ran into each other before!
Katie	Right? That's so weird.
Zac	Well, it's nice to finally meet you.
Katie	Same here.

True or False

1. Katie and Zac are meeting for the first time. .... True / False
2. Katie and Marissa met in Elementary school. .... True / False
3. Marissa and Zac met in Elementary school. .... True / False

Useful Expressions

1. I want to introduce you to my friend, Zac.
   - This is my friend, Zac.
   - Have you guys met before?

2. It's nice to meet you.
   - I'm so glad to meet you. / so good to meet you.
   - I've heard so much about you!
   - We meet at last.

READING 1

Meeting for the First Time

Fill in the blanks

Shake hands	cheek	first impression	smile

Meeting someone for the first time can be nerve-racking. Different people have different ways of greeting one another. In some cultures, people kiss on the _____________. This is a very common greeting in European countries. In North America and Australia, it is more common to _____________ as a introductory greeting. It's a friendly way to say "Nice to meet you." A good way to make a good _____________ when meeting someone new is to be kind and courteous. And always remember to be friendly and to _____________!

KEY-WORDS

shake hands: 손을 흔들다 **introductory**: 소개의 **common**: 보통의, 흔한, 공통의
courteous: 예의바른, 정중한 **cheek**: 뺨, 볼 **first impression**: 첫인상

READING 2

Sports & extracurriculars in schools

In America, students in school focus a lot on sports. They spend seven hours in school and afterwards their afternoons are dedicated to extracurricular activities. Oftentimes, these activities are athletics. Many students choose to do sports such as American football or lacrosse. These types of sports can help them get scholarships for college. If a student is very good at a sport, they can apply for government-funded money to help them pay for college. It is expected that they continue to play their sport in college. In order to play on a sports team in high school and in college, students have to maintain good grades. They have to be diligent about completing their homework. If a student falls behind in school, they can no longer play their sport. Sports are one of the many accomplishments a student can focus on in high school.

For students who are more interested in the arts, a popular extracurricular activity is participating in the school musical. Theatre and musicals give a place for people with many different interests and abilities to get involved. Aside from performers - singers, dancers, and actors - a musical production also needs technicians to run lights and sound, designers to design the set, and woodworkers to build and paint the set.

On top of this, a musical also needs costumers and makeup artists. They need someone to build the props that the actors will use on stage. They need a director and a managerial staff. Not to mention, a musical needs musicians! It's an extracurricular activity where anyone with any set of skills can find a place.

* **lacrosse**: 라크로스
각각 10명의 선수로 이뤄진 두 팀이 그물채 같은 것으로 공을 던지거나 잡으며 하는 하키 비슷한 경기

COMPREHENSION

1. In America, why are the students dedicated to extracurricular activities?
2. What do the students do to play on a sports team in high school and in college?
3. What is the popular extracurricular activity for students who are more interested in the arts?
4. Are musicians the only important part of musicals?

SUMMARY DISCUSSION QUESTIONS

1. How do you introduce yourself?
2. What are your extracurricular hobbies?
3. What can you do to make a good first impression?

Grammar+

I've known (I have known) you both for such a long time.

나는 너희 둘 모두 꽤 오랫동안 알고 지냈다.

현재완료: 주어+have+과거분사

과거에 발생한 일이 그것으로 그치지 않고 현재까지 이어지는 경우 현재완료 형태를 사용한다.
(Extra unit 참고)

KEY-WORDS

dedicated to: ~에 전념하는, 헌신하는 **extracurricular**: 정식 학과 이외의, 과외의, 본업 외의
oftentimes: [=often] 흔히, 자주, 보통 **athletics**: 육상, 운동(육상) 경기 **scholarship**: 장학금
such as: ~와 같은, 예를 들어 **in order to**: ~ 하기 위하여 **accomplishment**: 업적, 재주, 기량
interested in: ~에 관심이 있는 **popular**: 인기있는, 대중적인, 많은 사람들이 공유하는, 일반적인
run: 운영하다, 달리다 **involve**: 참여시키다, 수반하다, 관련시키다 **theatre**: [=theater] 극장, 공연장, 연극
participate: 참가하다, 참여하다 **performer**: 연기자, 연주자 **aside**: 이외에, 따로, 한쪽으로
technician: 기술자, 기사 **on top of**: 이외에, ~외에 **managerial**: 관리의, 운영의 **skill**: 기량, 기술
not to mention: ~ 말할 것도 없고, 물론이고

UNIT

02

Offering Congratulations

WARM-UP

Ⓐ Congratulations!

Ⓑ Thank you! This is great!!

GUESS

- What do you see in the picture?
- What might they be celebrating?

DIALOGUE

Amanda	Hi Melissa! I have a big announcement. I wanted to tell you in-person.
Melissa	Oh my god! What is it?
Amanda	I'll tell you, but it's still a secret from our other friends.
Melissa	Okay, I promise not to say anything.
Amanda	I'm pregnant!
Melissa	Wow! That is so exciting! I'm so happy for you!
Amanda	Thanks! My husband and I have been trying for a while. We are so happy.
Melissa	That is such great news. Is it a boy or a girl?
Amanda	We don't know yet. But I'm hoping for a girl!
Melissa	Well, as long as the baby is happy and healthy.
Amanda	Of course! I'm so glad to have your support.
Melissa	Please let me know when you have your baby shower. I want to get something really special for you and your new family.
Amanda	Thanks Melissa, that is so sweet! My baby can't wait to meet their new aunt.
Melissa	Aw, I promise I'll be the best aunt ever.

* **in-person** 직접

True or False

1. Melissa is having a baby. .... True / False

2. The baby is a girl. .... True / False

3. Melissa will be an aunt. .... True / False

Useful Expressions

1. I have a big announcement.

   – I have something to tell you.

   – I have an update.

2. I'm so happy for you.

   – Good for you.

   – That's great / amazing / awesome!

READING 1

A New Job

Fill in the blanks

anxious	promotion	coworkers	well-wishes

Jim just received a ______________ at work. Congratulations Jim! His co-workers will miss him, but they all agree that he deserves the ______________ and are happy for him. Jim feels excited and . He's going to be getting a raise, which is great. But, he is nervous about learning a new job. He really wants to do well. His ______________ signed a card for him filled with ______________. "We're all so happy for you!" they write. They hope he succeeds in his new position and comes to visit them from time to time. Jim will be missed.

KEY-WORDS

promotion: 승진, 진급, 승격 **deserve**: …할 만하다, …받을 가치가 있다
anxious: 걱정스러운, 불안한, 염려되는 **position**: 직책, 지위, 입장 **from time to time**: 가끔, 이따금
coworker: 동료, 함께 일하는 사람 **well-wish**: 호의

READING 2

Getting Married

In western cultures, getting married comes with many celebrations. Not only to people congratulate the bride and groom on their wedding day, they have multiple celebratory parties leading up to "the big day." It's common for friends of the bride to throw a big party for her a few weeks leading up to the wedding. They take the bride out to a nice restaurant and celebrate with champagne. They offer her congratulations and celebrate one last hurrah with her. As for the groom, he also has a big party a few weeks before the wedding with his friends. They have a night on the town and congratulate him on finding his bride-to-be.

On the wedding day, people toast the bride and groom and offer them congratulations and best wishes. Some people offer them advice, others offer some memories or kind words. They also give money or a gift. In return, the bridge and groom provide their guests with a meal, an open bar, and a night of dancing and celebration. Congrats to the newlyweds!

COMPREHENSION

1. What celebrations do brides and grooms have in western cultures?

2. How is this different from how your country celebrates a wedding?

3. What things do people say during a toast?

SUMMARY DISCUSSION QUESTIONS

1. What are some things we offer congratulations for?

2. What are some big life events you've experienced?

3. What do you think about western wedding culture?

4. Have you ever gotten a promotion? If so, how did you feel about it?

Grammar+

I promise not to say anything.

아무것도 말하지 않을 것을 약속하다.

to부정사: to+동사원형

동사원형이 to를 가짐으로써 명사의 역할을 한다.
say 말하다 – to say 말하는 것 (Extra unit 참고)

KEY-WORDS

get married: 결혼하다 **bride**: 신부 **groom**: 신랑 **multiple**: 복합의, 다수의, 다양한
celebratory: 기념[축하]하는 **lead up to**: …까지 인도하다, ~로 통하다
offer: 제공하다, …을 권하다 **last hurrah**: 마지막 시도[노력], 최후의 일
toast: ~를 위해 축배를 들다, 건배하다 **newlywed**: 신혼부부

UNIT

03

TV Shows / Entertainment

WARM-UP

Ⓐ What should we watch tonight?

Ⓑ It's up to you!

GUESS

- What do you see in the picture?
- What might they be watching?

DIALOGUE

Kate Hey, so what did you think of Squid Game?

Avery Oh man! I binge-watched the whole thing last weekend. What a ride!

Kate I know! I couldn't believe the ending.

Avery The marble episode was devastating. It was so hard to watch. I really got attached to some of the characters.

Kate I know, it was so disturbing. I had a hard time watching it too.

Avery And I couldn't believe the ending too!

Kate I know, I did not see it coming. And it's obvious they're going to make a second season.

Avery Yes, but they shouldn't. They should just leave it as it is.

Kate I agree.

Avery Anyway, I need a break from sad TV now. I want to watch something more up-beat next.

Kate Me too. Any suggestions?

Avery I've heard 'The Good Doctor' is good.

Kate Okay! I'll check it out.

* **binge watch**: 몰아서 보다
폭음, 폭식이라는 의미의 binge와 본다는 뜻의 watch가 결합된 용어

True or False

1. Avery watched the entire show in one weekend. ································ True / False

2. Kate and Avery will watch another sad / serious TV show next. ················ True / False

3. Kate and Avery both enjoyed the TV show. ···································· True / False

Useful Expressions

1. What did you think?
   - Do you have any idea on ~ ?
   - How do you like it?

2. Any suggestions?
   - Do you have any suggestions?
   - Do you have any recommendations for me?

READING 1

eBooks

Fill in the blanks

expand	fingertips	tablet	bookshelf

Have you ever tried an eBook? It's a device that allows you to read books electronically. It resembles a ____________. You swipe your finger across the screen to turn the pages of the book. You can download thousands of books. Any book you can think of is at your ____________. Many eBook devices have a free book section where you can download and read classics such as "Moby Dick" and "Pride & Prejudice" at no cost. You can reduce the size of your ____________ and at the same time ____________ your library. Though an eBook might not feel the same as holding a book in your hands and turning the pages, the possibilities of what you can read are endless. The words on the page stay the same.

* **Moby Dick**: [백경] 미국의 소설가 H.멜빌의 장편소설
* **Pride & Prejudice**: [오만과 편견] 영국의 소설가 제인 오스틴의 장편소설

KEY-WORDS

device: 장치, 설비 **allow**: 허락하다, 허가하다 **electronically**: 전자적으로
resemble: …와 닮다, …와 공통점이 있다 **reduce**: 줄이다, 축소하다 **at the same time**: 동시에
though: …이긴 하지만, …이지만 **swipe**: 쓸어 넘기다 **endless**: 끝없는, 무한한

READING 2

Podcasts

Podcasts are a great way to get new information, catch up on news, or listen to creative stories. People can listen to podcasts through an app on their phone, on their laptop, or through any other streaming device. It's common for people to listen to podcasts while driving or while performing mundane tasks.

One popular category of podcasts is 'True Crime.' True Crime podcasts detail a real event, often times an assault or murder, either episode-by-episode or through a series of episodes. This genre of podcast has become very popular and therefore more and more podcasts about true crime are being produced.

Some true crime listeners have even been able to provide clues to police, while listening to a podcast, which ended up helping to crack some of the unsolved crimes.

Another popular type of podcast are news podcasts. They are a really great way to stay up to date on current events. Different news channels offer different types of news stories and categories. There are also various op-ed or opinion-based editorial podcasts available.

Overall, podcasts are a great way to stay entertained on a drive to work or while doing chores around the house. They can be informative or can be used strictly for entertainment. They are a new way to enjoy even more content in our technologically expanding world.

COMPREHENSION

1. Why do people listen to podcasts?

2. What are some popular types of podcasts?

3. Where do people typically listen to podcasts?

4. What types of podcasts are you interested in?

SUMMARY DISCUSSION QUESTIONS

1. What types of TV shows do you enjoy?

2. What are some other types of entertainment that you enjoy?

3. What is your favorite form of entertainment and why?

4. Have you ever listened to a podcast? If so, what was it about?

Grammar+

It was so hard to watch.

보기가 정말 힘들었어.

to부정사의 명사적 용법– 주어 it(가주어) ~ to–v(진주어)

to부정사가 주어로 쓰여 길어질 경우 보통 가주어 it 을 쓰고 to부정사구는 뒤로 보낸다. (Extra unit 참고)

KEY-WORDS

catch up: 밀린 것을 따라잡다 **creative**: 창조적인, 창의적인 **through**: ~통하여, 관통하여
while: …하는 동안 **mundane**: 재미없는, 일상적인 **assault**: 강습, 습격, 강렬한 비난
murder: 살해하다, 살해, 살인 **either A or B**: A이거나 B인 **genre**: 장르, 유형, 양식
provide: 주다, 공급하다 **clue**: 단서 **ended up ~ing**: 결국 ~하게 되다 **op–ed**: 기명 논평 페이지
Overall: 전체의, 종합적인, 종합적으로, 전반적으로 **content**: 내용물
informative: 유익한, 유용한 정보를 주는 **strictly**: 엄격하게, 엄밀히 정확히

UNIT

04

Eating Out

WARM-UP

A Would you like anything else?
B We'll all set!
A Perfect. Enjoy your meal.

GUESS

- What do you see in the picture?
- What types of restaurants do you enjoy?

DIALOGUE

Waitress Hi, welcome to Bella Italia. I'm Tania, I'll be your server today. Can I start you off with something to drink?

Amanda Actually, we haven't had a chance to look at the drink menu yet.

Waitress Oh, okay, I'll give you a few minutes to look it over and I'll come back and take your order.

Mark Would you bring us a few waters in the meantime?

Waitress Of course!

Amanda So Mark, what are you thinking?

Mark I might order a beer, how about you?

Amanda I'm thinking about a glass of wine. I want to see what our waitress recommends.

Waitress Here are your waters, have you had a chance to decide what you'd like to drink?

Mark I'll have a Blue Moon.

Waitress Sure! And for you?

Amanda I'd like a red wine, which do you recommend?

Waitress Well, are you looking for something sweet or more dry?

Amanda I'd like a dry wine.

Waitress Then I'd recommend our house Pinot Noir.

Amanda Sounds great, I'll have that.

Waitress Wonderful. I'll put those in and I'll be back in a few to take your orders.

Amanda Do you want to share an appetizer?

Mark Sure! What are you thinking?

Amanda I thought the burrata looked really good.

Mark Oo, that does look good. Let's order that.

Amanda Great, do you know what you want for your meal?

Mark Yes, I'm ready to order.

Waitress Here's your beer and your glass of wine. Can I put in any appetizers for you guys?

Mark Yes, we'll have the burrata.

Waitress Great choice. And are you ready to order?

Amanda Yes, I'll have the rizotto.

Waitress Okay.

Mark And I'll have the filet minion.

Waitress Great, would you like soup or salad with that?

Mark I'll have the soup.

Waitress Sounds great, I'll go ahead and put that in for you. Do you need anything else right now?

Amanda We're all set!

True or False

1. Amanda and Mark are ready to order right away. ································ True / False
2. Amanda and Mark order an appetizer. ··· True / False
3. Mark will have a salad with his meal. ··· True / False

Useful Expressions

1. Which do you recommend?
   - What's your most popular ~?
   - What's good for sharing?
   - what's good today?
2. I'll have the soup.
   - I'd like the soup.

READING 1

Cooking a Simple Meal

Fill in the blanks

serving bowl	pinch	simmer	tender

Spaghetti with tomato sauce is a simple dish to make. First, fill a big pot with water. Throw in a ____________ of salt. While the water heats up, take out a second, smaller pot. Pour in your tomato sauce and let it ____________. When the water from your big pot boils, put in the spaghetti. After about seven minutes, your spaghetti should be nice and ____________. Find a strainer and pour your spaghetti out of the pot and into the strainer. Then, put your spaghetti into a ____________. Pour your tomato sauce onto your spaghetti. Grab two mixing spoons and mix your sauce evenly in with your spaghetti. Lastly, sprinkle on some parmesan cheese and serve. You now have a delicious Italian meal!

KEY-WORDS

heat up: 뜨거워지다, 따뜻해지다 **Pour**: 따르다, 쏟다, 붓다 **strainer**: 체
evenly: 평평하게, 균등하게, 균일하게, 고르게 **sprinkle**: 뿌리다, 끼얹다 **tender**: 부드러운, 씹기 쉬운
simmer: 부글부글[지글지글] 끓다 **pinch**: 꼬집다, [두 손가락으로] 집다

READING 2

Eating at a Fancy Restaurant

Different cultures have different manners for eating in a high-end restaurant. In western cultures, dining out at a nice restaurant is a time-consuming and expensive activity. It's something that people generally don't do often and is meant for special occasions.

When people go to a nice restaurant, there is an expected dress-code. Jeans and spaghetti straps are frowned upon. Usually, an upscale restaurant has a policy requiring men to wear a suit jacket. Some restaurants have extra suit jackets on hand to lend out to patrons who don't have their own.

When eating at a high-end restaurant, customers order their food and expect that their food takes 20-30 minutes to arrive. Oftentimes, they will order a beverage and order an appetizer. Typically, there is also bread on the table for patrons to eat while they wait for their next course. Usually, the meal will end with an option for dessert.

At the end of the meal, the waiter brings the check. In western culture, it's customary to tip the waiter 20% of the cost of the meal for good service. Overall, the experience of eating out at a nice restaurant can take up to one or two hours. The time should be filled with delicious food and good conversation.

COMPREHENSION

1. What are you expected to wear when going out to eat at a nice place?

2. What are the typical courses at a high-end restaurant?

3. How does tipping work?

4. How is eating out in a western country different from eating out in your country?

SUMMARY DISCUSSION QUESTIONS

1. What type of restaurants do you enjoy?

2. How is eating out different in different cultures?

3. Why do people tip in some countries?

4. What meal can you cook yourself? How do you make it?

Grammar+

I'd like a red wine, which do you recommend?

저는 레드와인을 원해요, 어떤 것을 추천하시나요?

would like to+동사원형

want와 비슷한 의미로도 쓰이며 '~하고 싶다, 원하다'는 의미를 가진다. (Extra unit 참고)

KEY-WORDS

high-end: 최고급의 **time-consuming** :시간이 걸리는, 시간을 낭비하는
generally: 일반적으로, 널리, 보통 **occasion**: 경우, 때, 기회, [특별한]행사 **dress-code**: 복장 규정
upscale: 풍부한, 고소득층에 속하는, 부자의 **patron**: 고객, 단골, 후원자
Typically: 보통,일반적으로, 전형적으로 **customary**: 습관적인, 재래의, 통례의, 관습상의

UNIT

05

Shopping

WARM-UP

Ⓐ Do you need help finding anything today?
Ⓑ I think I'm all set, thanks!

GUESS

- What do you see in the picture?
- What type of store is she shopping in?

DIALOGUE

Store Employee	Hi there, are you finding everything okay today?
Ashley	Yes, I'm okay for now.
Store Employee	Okay, great. If there's anything I can help you with, please let me know.
Ashley	Thanks. Actually, I do have a question. Do you have any more of these shirts in a larger size?
Store Employee	Unfortunately, if it's not on the floor, that means we're sold out. We don't carry extra stock in the back. However, if you check our online store, they might have a smaller size in stock.
Ashley	Okay, thanks. Where can I go if I need to make a return?
Store Employee	The return desk is right over there.
Ashley	Thanks for your help.
Return Desk Employee	Hello, ma'am, can I help you?
Ashley	Yes, I'd like to return this dress. It doesn't fit.
Return Desk Employee	Sure, I can help you with that. Do you have the receipt?
Ashley	I don't have it anymore actually.
Return Desk Employee	Alright, let me see what I can do for you. Hmm, it seems like you can return the item, but I'll have to give you store credit only.
Ashley	Okay, that's fine.
Return Desk Employee	Okay then. This return will be $28.36 in store credit. It's here on this card. Thank you for shopping with us.

Ashley	Okay, thanks a lot.
Return Desk Employee	Have a nice day.
Ashley	You as well.

True or False

1. Ashley is looking for a larger shirt than the ones on display. ···················· True / False

2. There are extra shirts in the back of the store. ································· True / False

3. Ashley is able to return her dress. ·· True / False

Useful Expressions

1. Can I help you find anything today?

   – May I help you?

   – How ca I help you?

   – Do you need anything?

   +) I'm just looking around. / I'm just browsing.

2. Do you have any more of these shirts in a larger size?

   – Does this come in size ~ [eg. 12,14] ?

   – I need this in a large.

3. I'd like to return this.

   – Can I get a refund on ~ ?

   – I'd like a refund on ~.

READING 1

The Mall

Fill in the blanks

retailers	discount	in-person	sales tax

Even though online-shopping is very popular, many people still prefer to do ______________ shopping. A common place for people to do their shopping is a shopping mall. These establishments host a variety of ______________. There are dozens of stores. There are clothing stores like JCPenney and video game stores like Game Shop. They also usually have electronics stores like Apple and jewelry stores like Zales.

Around the holidays, many stores offer ______________. People can buy items at a lower cost. It's common for many shoppers to wait to buy certain items until they go on sale. When shopping online or in stores, people often forget about ______________. People don't always realize that the item they purchase will be slightly more expensive than the price listed on the price tag. Hopefully they have some extra money with them just in case!

KEY-WORDS

even though: 비록 ~일지라도, 설사 ~이라고 할지라도 **prefer to**: ~보다 선호하다
retailer: 소매상인, 소매업자 **discount**: 할인 **in-person**: 직접 **sales tax**: 판매세
establishment: 기관, 시설 **variety**: 변화, 다양성 **dozen**: 다스, 12개짜리 묶음, 여러 개
realize: 깨닫다, 알아차리다, 실현하다 **purchase**: 사다, 구입하다, 매수하다 **slightly**: 약간, 조금

READING 2

Amazon: Pros & Cons

Online shopping has never been easier thanks to Amazon. Amazon, which first began as an online bookstore, has become the largest online store in the world. It hosts over 1.4 million retailers. Amazon sells toys, clothes, electronics, and even groceries and foods. There is very little that can't be bought on Amazon. They even have free shipping options in exchange for an annual subscription to Amazon Prime, a benefit to shoppers who use the site often. Amazon ships very quickly, often overnight. The company has given a market to many businesses world-wide who otherwise would not have access to international growth. It has also created many jobs and has helped grow the economy.

However, there is a dark side to Amazon. While Amazon is a billion dollar company whose CEO is currently the richest man alive, it's workers do not fare as well. Amazon has been known to push it's workers, who make minimum wages which are not livable, to work extreme hours. They are given little breaks and are barely meeting labor laws. Their worker's unions are often bought out and silenced. Additionally, due to Amazon's convenience and fast delivery service, they have made it almost impossible for any other market to compete with. They have become an unstoppable monopoly. Many small businesses have gone out of business because they have lost their customers to the low prices and convenience Amazon is able to offer due to its sheer size and reach.

Amazon has been able to drive down market sales and offer quick and affordable service and product to its customers. However, it comes at a huge cost to competing businesses as well as its employees.

COMPREHENSION

1. What is a workers union? Are you part of a union?
2. What are the benefits of Amazon?
3. What are the downsides of Amazon?
4. Do you shop online? Why or why not?

SUMMARY DISCUSSION QUESTIONS

1. Do you enjoy shopping?
2. What are the pros and cons of shopping online? Shopping in-person?
3. What are your favorite stores and what do these stores sell?
4. Do you know anyone with a shopping addiction? What are the repercussions?

Grammar+

If you check our online store, they might have a smaller size in stock.

만약 당신이 우리의 온라인 스토어를 확인한다면 그들은 아마 작은 사이즈 재고가 있을 거예요.

if 단순 조건문: if+주어 +동사, 주어+조동사+동사

'만약 ~한다면'이라는 뜻으로 실제로 발생 가능한 일을 가정할 때 쓴다. (Extra unit 참고)

KEY-WORDS

just in case: 만약을 위해서, ~한 경우에 한해서 **pros and cons**: 장단점, 찬반[찬부] 양론
thanks to: ~ 덕분에 **ship**: 수송하다 **grocery**: 식료품 **overnight**: 하룻밤 사이의, 밤을 새는, 일박의
world-wide: 세계적인 **otherwise**: 다른점에서는, 다른 **access**: 접근, 출입 **growth**: 성장, 발육, 발전
economy: 경제, 절약 **labor**: 노동, 근로, 노동하다 **convenience**: 편리, 편의
compete: 겨루다, 경쟁하다 **unstoppable**: 멈출 수 없는, 제지할 수 없는 **monopoly**: 독점, 전매
go out of: ~에서 없어지다, ~을 떠나다 **sheer**: 순전한, 순수한
affordable: 알맞은, 줄 수 있는, 입수 가능한 **as well as** :~에 더하여, 게다가, -과 마찬가지로 잘

UNIT

06

At the Airport

WARM-UP

A Do you have your boarding pass?

B Yes, here it is.

GUESS

- What do you see in the picture?
- What items do you need to bring with you to the airport?

DIALOGUE

Ticket Agent Passport and ID please.

Sam Here.

Ticket Agent Where are you flying to today?

Sam I'm going to Los Angeles.

Ticket Agent And what brings you to Los Angeles?

Sam I'm visiting my cousin for the holidays.

Ticket Agent That's nice. Are you a member of our frequent flyer program?

Sam No, I'm not.

Ticket Agent Would you like to join for $50? You'll receive priority seating on all flights and you'll be able to log miles on all of our flights and our sister flights including today's flight.

Sam No thanks, I don't fly often enough.

Ticket Agent Not a problem. Would you like a window seat or an aisle seat for your flight today?

Sam I'd like an aisle seat.

Ticket Agent Okay great. Are you checking any bags with us today?

Sam Yes, I have one bag.

Ticket Agent Put in on the weight belt please.

Sam Sure.

Ticket Agent Sir, your bag is over our weight capacity of 50 pounds. You can either pay an additional fee or you can remove some items from your bag.

Sam What is the fee?

Ticket Agent $25.

Sam Okay. Do you take credit?

Ticket Agent Yes sir.

Sam Alright.

Ticket Agent Great. You are all set. Here is your boarding pass. You'll head over to Gate 23. Don't forget to pick up your luggage in baggage claim in Los Angeles.

Sam Alright, have a good one.

Ticket Agent You too, sir.

True or False

1. Sam has to pay a fee because his baggage is overweight. .... True / False
2. Sam will join the mileage program. .... True / False
3. Sam is visiting his parents for the holidays. .... True / False

Useful Expressions

1. Sir, your bag is over our weight capacity of 50 pounds.
   - Your bag is overwight.
   - your carry–on is too large.

2. I'd prefer an aisle / window seat.
   - Can I have an a(n) window / aisle seat?
   - I'd like the emergency exit row.
   - Can I have an empty seat next to me?

READING 1

Airlines Saving Money

Fill in the blanks

profit	in-flight	airlines	checked bag

These days, airlines are doing more and more to save money. Seats are smaller in size, leg room has been reduced, the aisles are narrower. This allows them to cram in a few more seats on the plane. Some airlines have even stopped handing out earbuds and blankets while some ______________ have eliminated the TV entertainment service from their seats. In order to watch the ______________ entertainment, you have to pay for the airplane's WiFi service and watch their entertainment through your smartphone or tablet. Some airlines have reduced the food portions that they give out to their customers. They no longer give one free ______________ per flight. Airlines are more and more about maximizing ______________ and reducing costs to save money.

KEY-WORDS

profit: 이익, 수익, 소득 **in-flight**: 비행중의 **airline**: 항공회사 **cram**: 억지로 채워넣다, 밀어넣다
hand out: 나눠주다, 배포하다 **eliminate**: 없애다, 제거하다, 탈락시키다
WiFi: wireless fidelity – 무선 데이터 전송 시스템 **maximizing** :극대화하는, 극한까지 확대하는

READING 2

Tips & Tricks at the Airport

Flying can be very stressful. Airports are busy and getting to your gate can be a hassle. However, there are some tips and tricks that can help make your airport experience a breeze.

Before you arrive at the airport, it's helpful if you're already checked in to your flight. Check-in online up to 24 hours before your flight. This way, when you arrive at the airport, you can skip the line and simply print your boarding pass at a kiosk. As you head to security, make sure you've removed any belts and jewelry beforehand. I hope you've worn slip-on shoes to the airport! As you get closer to the security check, remove your shoes. Once you place your things in the bucket and put it on the conveyor belt, walk through the metal detector with ease. Gather up your items as they pass through security and slip on your shoes. From there, simply head to your gate, grab a cup of coffee, and relax.

Once you board the plane, if you can, store your items under your seat instead of in the overhead bin. This will make for a swift exit from the plane once you land. I hope you brought your headphones! These days, many flights no longer give our headphones to passengers and if they do, they're very uncomfortable. Bring your own headphones, plug in, and tune out. Alcohol is free during international flights. When the drink cart comes around, don't be shy about asking for a glass of wine to go with your meal. It'll help relax you. As you touch down safely, stay sharp and try to get ahead of the crowd. Remember, you don't have to search for any of their things from the overhead bins, they're right at the tips of your toes. Grab and go!

COMPREHENSION

1. What should you do before arriving at the airport?
2. What items do you have to remove before going through security?
3. Why does the writer suggest not storing your items in the overhead bin?
4. What do you do to relax during a flight?

SUMMARY DISCUSSION QUESTIONS

1. Have you traveled on an airplane? Where did you go?
2. What items do you need to bring with you to the airport?
3. What is the most stressful part of traveling?
4. What can travelers do to make their experience less stressful?

Grammar+

I'm visiting my cousin for the holidays.

나는 휴가중에 내 사촌들을 만날 거예요.

현재진행형: 주어+be+현재분사

일반적으로 현재진행형은 '~하는 중이다의 의미로 지금 진행중인 일을 나타내지만 위와 같이 가까운 미래를 나타내기도 한다.

KEY-WORDS

hassle: 귀찮은 상황, 재촉하다, 들볶다 **kiosk**: 터치스크린 방식의 정보전달 시스템인 무인단말기
beforehand: 미리, 사전에 **slip-on**: 손쉽게 입고 벗을 수 있는 **security**: 안전, 보안
instead of: ~대신에 **headphones**: 헤드폰

UNIT

07

At a Hotel

WARM-UP

Ⓐ Hello, I have a reservation under my name.

Ⓑ Great! Let me just find your reservation in our system.

GUESS

- What do you see in the picture?
- What will the customer have to provide the receptionist in order to check-in?

DIALOGUE

John Hi, good afternoon.

Receptionist Good afternoon, how can I help you?

John I have a reservation under the name John Adams.

Receptionist Sure, can I take a look at your ID?

John Absolutely, here you are.

Receptionist Great, thanks. Okay, I've found your name in the system. You're staying two nights with us?

John Yes.

Receptionist Alright. King size bed?

John That is correct.

Receptionist Okay, great. You'll be in room 201. Check in is at 3pm and check out is 11am. There is a pool on the first floor and we have a restaurant down the hall. It's open from 11am-10pm.

John Okay, thank you.

Receptionist Here is your keycard. You'll go up the elevator to the second floor. It's down the hall to the left. Any questions?

John Yes, actually. What do you recommend I do while I'm in town?

Receptionist There's a really nice art museum in town and there's a nice nature walk in Greensboro Park.

John That sounds great. Thank you for the recommendation.

Receptionist Sure! Enjoy your stay.

John Will do. Thanks again.

True or False

1. John would like some recommendations from the receptionist. ················ True / False

2. John can eat breakfast at the hotel. ·· True / False

3. John can go swimming at the hotel. ·· True / False

Useful Expressions

1. I have a reservation.

   – My reservation is under [name]

2. Can I take a look at your ID?

   – May I see your passport and a credit card?

3. You're staying two nights with us?

   – How long will you be stayig?

   – What day will you be checking out?

READING 1

A New Hotel

Fill in the blanks

luxury	workout center	attraction	facilities

A new hotel is opening up in downtown Hartford. It will be 30 stories tall. It will have a swimming pool as well as a heated pool and a jacuzzi. It will also have a sauna. In addition, the hotel will have a ______________ with top-of-the-line equipment. It will be open 24 hours to all guests of the hotel. The hotel will have a 5-star restaurant and bar that will be open to hotel guests as well as to the public. Although the hotel will cater to high-end guests offering ______________ suits with designer linens and ______________, there will be options available for guests who are looking for something more affordable. The hotel hopes to become a sought out ______________ for guests coming to Hartford and aspires to be an asset of the city.

KEY-WORDS

luxury: 사치의, 고급의, 사치, 호사 **workout center**: 헬스장 **attraction**: 매력 **facility**: 편의 시설
jacuzzi: 목욕탕 **top-of-the-line**: 최고급품의, 최신식의, 무리 중에서 최고 **equipment**: 장비, 설비
cater: 음식물을 조달[장만]하다 **linen**: 리넨 제품(침대 시트, 베갯잇 등), 아마 섬유
seek out: (오랜동안 공들여) 찾아다닌 끝에 찾아내다 / 구하다 / 발견하다 **aspire to**: ~을 갈망하다

READING 2

A Pamphlet from a Hotel in Connecticut

Connecticut is a small state in New England. Is in part of the North-Eastern region of the U.S.A. Connecticut borders three other states: New York, Massachusetts, and Rhode Island. Connecticut has a squarish shape. The fourth side of the square borders the ocean. It's called 'The Connecticut Sound.' Though the state is very populated everywhere, a majority of the population live on the coast.

There are many sailboats and yachts to be seen in any of Connecticut's coastal towns. In summer, people sail and do other water sports and activities.

It's a very popular summer destination for travelers. Some of the most popular towns to visit are Mystic and New Haven. These towns have historic buildings and have public access to beaches.

Connecticut is also home to one of the most famous universities in the country: Yale University. It is located in New Haven. Along with being known for the coast and the university, New Haven is also known for its pizza! Former President Bill Clinton, who attended Yale, used to have pizza from New Haven flown into the White House whenever he craved it.

Connecticut also closely borders New York City. Many people who can't afford to live right in NYC come to live in Connecticut for a more affordable, slower-paced life. Connecticut has a lot to offer to its residents and to travelers!

COMPREHENSION

1. How many states does Connecticut border?

a. One
b. Two
c. Three
d. Four

2. Why do people come to live in Connecticut?

a. It's fast – paced
b. It's expensive
c. The coast
d. Good schools

3. Connecticut is:

a. A state boarding the coast
b. A land – locked state
c. A big mid – western state
d. A warm state in the south

4. This passage explains:

a. Why people like living on a state that borders the ocean
b. Reasons people live in Connecticut
c. Different things Connecticut has to offer
d. Good universities in Connecticut

5. What do you like to see when you're visiting a new place?

6. What qualities do you look for in a hotel?

SUMMARY DISCUSSION QUESTIONS

1. What is the process of checking into a hotel?

2. What facilities do you look for in selecting a hotel?

3. What do you expect to find in your hotel room?

4. In your opinion, what makes the difference between a good hotel and a bad one?

Grammar+

What do you recommend I do while I'm in town?

제가 이 곳에 있는 동안 무엇을 하기를 추천하시나요?

접속사 while: while+주어+동사 ~

while은 '~하는 동안' 이라는 뜻으로 전치사 for, during과 비슷한 의미를 가지지만 전치사는 명사를 목적어로 갖는 반면 while은 접속사이므로 문장형태를 쓰는 것에 주의한다.

KEY-WORDS

asset: 자산, 재산 **pamphlet**: 팸플릿, 소책자 **border**: 국경지방, 경계, 테두리 **squarish**: 네모난, 네모진 **majority**: 대부분, 대다수 **destination**: 목적지, 행선지 **be located in**: ~에 위치하다 **be known for**: ~로 알려져 있다 **former**: 전의, 앞의 **used to**: ~하곤 했다 **crave**: 열망하다 **resident**: 거주자

UNIT

08

Having a Party

WARM-UP

Ⓐ Happy birthday Julia! How old are you turning?
Ⓑ I'm turning 30! I can't believe it!

GUESS

- What do you see in the picture?
- How do people celebrate a birthday?

DIALOGUE

Ally Hey Brian, I've been thinking, I think we should throw a surprise birthday party for Sarah.

Brian Really? That's a good idea! I'm in, let's plan her party.

Ally Okay, well, where should we have it?

Brian I don't mind hosting the party at my house, I have lots of room.

Ally Okay, great. We can get catering for the food. Does Sarah have any allergies?

Brian Hmm, not that I know of. I will ask her.

Ally Okay, but don't give away the surprise.

Brian I won't. Should we make it a BYOB event or should we provide beverages?

Ally I think since we're throwing the party, we should provide all the food and drinks.

Brian That works. We'll also have to provide entertainment. Games?

Ally How about a band?

Brian That sounds expensive. Let's just play music through our phones.

Ally Good plan. Okay, well this is a good start. Let's touch base next week.

Brian Sounds great, talk soon!

* **BYOB**: Bring Your Own Booze(Bottle)

True or False

1. Ally and Brian will hire a band for the party. .... True / False

2. Brian and Ally will cook food for their guests. .... True / False

3. Sarah does not have any food allergies. .... True / False

Useful Expressions

1. Let's plan a party.
   - Let's make a plan for the party.
   - Why don't we plan a party.

2. Let's touch base soon.
   - Let's talk again soon.
   - Hit me up. (가까운 사이의 격식이 없는 말)

READING 1

Christmas

Fill in the blanks

presents	mistletoe	Christianity	jolly

In many parts of the world, Christmas is the biggest holiday of the year. People decorate their homes, put up a Christmas tree and string it up with lights, and spend lots of money on ____________ to place under the tree. Some people even hang ____________ in their home. As tradition goes, if you're caught standing under the mistletoe with someone else, you must kiss. Christmas is a time to celebrate family and friends and to give to charities and people in need.

However, Christmas's real purpose is tied to Christianity. It's a religious holiday celebrated primarily by followers of the church. However, overtime, the popularity of the holiday caught on and now it's celebrated by people who are not-religious as well.

Around December, people are said to have 'Christmas spirit.' There's said to be a ____________ feeling in the air. It can almost be described as 'joyous.' Children are excited and people are feeling generous and giving. Many people throw Christmas parties or celebrations. It's a magical holiday for the people who celebrate.

KEY-WORDS

decorate: 꾸미다, 장식하다 **present**: 선물 **mistletoe**: 겨우살이 **charity**: 자애, 자선, 너그러움, 관용
purpose: 목적, 의도 **christianity**: 기독교 **religious**: 종교의, 종교적인 **catch on**: 이해하다, 유행하다
jolly: 명랑한, 즐거운 **generous**: 관대한, 아량있는

READING 2

A Golden Anniversary

Do you know of any couples who have been married for over 50 years? If so, you know of someone who has celebrated their golden anniversary. A golden anniversary is celebrated by couples on the 50th year of their marriage. Typically, couples who have made it to their golden year are in their 70s or older. It's a cause for celebration.

Sometimes, family and friends will throw a party for a couple who is celebrating this huge milestone in their marriage. Children, family, and friends might organize an event for the couple. They might reserve a nice space, have catering come and prepare delicious food for the guests, and hire a DJ to play music for the couple and guests to dance to. In some instances, there might be an open bar. Guests of the celebration might tell stories about the couple and share memories of them. The couple might share a special slow dance together.

In some cases, guests might even bring gifts to the couple. Others might organize a special album or book filled with photos, letters, and other memorabilia that signifies the couple's marriage. It serves as a keepsake for the couple and the special day they shared. Let's hope we all get to celebrate our own golden anniversary!

COMPREHENSION

1. What is a golden anniversary?

2. What are some things a couple might do at a party for their anniversary?

3. What is a keepsake? Do you have any?

4. Do you celebrate big anniversaries in your country? If so, how?

SUMMARY DISCUSSION QUESTIONS

1. What kinds of parties do people throw?

2. What do people enjoy doing at a party?

3.Have you ever thrown a party before? What did you do to plan it?

4.What do you normally do on your birthday?

Grammar+

We'll also have to provide entertainment.

우리는 재미도 제공해야 해.

의무: have to / has to+동사원형

must와 같이 '~해야 한다'라는 의미의 강한 의무를 나타내지만 부정형은 의미가 전혀 달라지므로 유의한다.

don't have to: ~할 필요가 없다

must not: ~해서는 안된다.

KEY-WORDS

anniversary: 기념일 **marriage**: 결혼, 결혼생활 **milestone**: 중요한 단계 **share**: 나누다, 공유하다

In some instance: 어떤 경우에는 **memorabilia**: 기록할 만한 사건 **keepsake**: 유품, 기념품

UNIT

09

Job Interview

WARM-UP

Ⓐ Why are you interested in this position?

Ⓑ I think the position sounds very exciting and I think I'd be great at it.

GUESS

- What do you see in the picture?
- What job do you think the man is applying for?

DIALOGUE

Lana Hi Dave, it's nice to meet you. Please take a seat.

Dave It's nice to meet you too. Thanks.

Lana So, first of all, tell me a little about yourself and your work history.

Dave Well, I'm a UCLA graduate with a degree in economics. I worked at an electrical company for ten years and I decided that I wanted to branch out and try something new.

Lana Okay, great. And what made you interested in the Sales & Marketing Management position here at Lieman's.

Dave Well, since I have a strong background in numbers and economic trends, I thought I'd be a good fit for the position. It's a step up from the position I was in last and feel I'm ready to take on a higher role. I really like the values of your company and I feel my background is strongly aligned with your core beliefs such as the drive to close the gender gap.

Lana That's great to hear. So Dave, if you are hired, what will you do to close the gender-wage gap?

Dave Well, I'd make a push to hire more women at the company and I would make sure that my hires were gender-balanced. I'd also fight for everyone on my team to make an equal salary.

Lana Good answer. What makes you a good fit for the position?

Dave I'm hard-working, determined, organized, and I have a background in studying economic trends which I believe can transfer well into sales and marketing.

Lana Alright! And what are your strengths as a team member?

Dave Well, I'm very good at delegating tasks. People tend to see me as a leader. I work well with others and strive to keep a positive work environment.

Lana That's very good to hear. Do you have any questions for me?

Dave Yes, what are the typical work hours?

Lana Our typical work hours are 9am to 5pm. There is some overtime opportunities but we encourage a healthy work-life balance among our staff, so we try not to have our workers do too much overtime.

Dave That sounds great.

Lana Yes. Okay, well if you don't have any questions, it was very nice to meet you, we will be in touch!

Dave Okay, great. I'm looking forward to hearing from you.

True or False

1. Dave is qualified for the position. ········ True / False

2. One of the coe beliefs of the company is gender equality. ········ True / False

3. Lana will hire Dave. ········ True / False

Useful Expressions

1. Tell me about yourself.

- Can you tell me aout yourself?
- What relevant experience do you have?
- What are your qualifications?

2. what made you interested in the Sales & Marketing Management position here at Lieman's.

- Why do you want this job?
- why do you want to work for Lieman's?

READING 1

My Qualifications

Fill in the blanks

prioritize	hard-worker	opportunity	double-check

What makes me the most qualified person for the position? First of all, I'm a very _______________. If given a task, I always make sure to complete it on time to the best of my ability. I _______________ my work and if needed, have it peer-reviewed before I turn it in. Second of all, I am very organized. I _______________ all of my tasks. I keep my desk clean and my files clean. I keep a good track of everything I do. Third of all, I work well with others. I believe that teamwork is very important and I always strive to create a safe and positive work environment for me and my coworkers. Lastly, I have over ten years experience in the field. I've worked in a similar position at a former company. However, I have always wanted to work for this company so when the position became available I jumped at the _______________ to apply.

KEY-WORDS

align: 나란히 만들다, 일직선으로 하다 **hire**: 고용하다 **strength**: 힘, 장점
prioritize: (계획 · 목표)에 우선 순위를 매기다; 우선시키다. **opportunity**: 기회, 호기; 행운; 가망
double-check: 다시 한 번 확인하다, 재확인하다. **peer review**: 동료심사
turn in: ~을 제출하다, 반납하다 **strive**: 노력하다

READING 2

Remote Interviews

Due to the Covid-19 pandemic, interview culture has changed. Before Covid, a virtual interview seemed impossible, but now it has become a common way for an employer to scope out potential employees. Many companies have various Zoom or remote interview processes.

Some companies will ask the potential hire to record a video of themselves answering preset questions. In these instances, there is no interviewer. The applicant simply receives a set of interview questions and submits a video of themselves answering them. This can be challenging for some as you receive no feedback during the interview process. It can seem awkward or uncomfortable. It also does not give the interviewee a chance to ask questions or interact with the company.

More commonly, applicants will be asked to participate in a live remote interview session. They will be sent a link, a date, and a time. The person applying for the job should have a good background and should dress professionally for the interview. The interviewer might invite others involved in the hiring process to join the call. This style of interview feels similar to a face-to-face interview. It takes place in real time and the potential hire has a chance to ask and answer questions and engage with the company. They can do this all from the comfort of their own home. Is there ever going back?

COMPREHENSION

1. What are the cons of doing a self-recorded interview?

2. How does a live remote interview work?

3. Why should you dress nicely for an interview even though it is remote?

4. Do you prefer remote interviews or in-person interviews? Why?

SUMMARY DISCUSSION QUESTIONS

1. What makes you a good candidate for a job?

2. Do you do well in interviews? Why or why not?

3. What can you improve about your interviewing skills?

4. What kinds of questions might an interviewer ask?

Grammar+

I have a background in studying economic trends <u>which</u> I believe can transfer well into sales and marketing.

저는 영업과 마케팅에 잘 접목할 수 있는 경제 동향에 대해 공부했습니다.

관계대명사 which

관계대명사 which는 접속사와 대명사 역할을 하며, 선행사가 사물이나 동물인 경우 사용한다. (Extra unit 참고)

KEY-WORDS

virtual: 실제상의, 실질적인, 사실상의 **scope out**: 자세히 살피다 **employee**: 고용인, 사용인, 종업원
preset: 미리 설치된 **submit**: 지시에 따르다 **awkward**: 거북한, 어색한
interviewee: 면접받는 사람, 면접 대상자 **face-to-face**: 정면으로 마주보는; 맞부딪치는

UNIT

10

Business

A I need to reschedule the meeting with our client today, something came up.

B Okay, no problem. I'll take care of it.

GUESS

- What do you see in the picture?
- What goes into running a business?

DIALOGUE

Mary	Hey Kayla, I've been thinking. We should go into business together.
Kayla	Really? What kind of business?
Mary	I was thinking, with your accounting skills and my baking skills, we could run a very successful bakery shop.
Kayla	A bakery, that sounds interesting. But do you think there is much demand for a new bakery in town? We'd be competing with "Little Miss Cupcake" on Main Street.
Mary	I thought of that too, but our bakery will be different. We will specialize in custom-made cakes and unique cookies. Since "Little Miss Cupcake" only sells cupcakes, we'll be cornering a new market.
Kayla	Wow, you've given this a lot of thought. If you do all the baking, what will I do with the business?
Mary	I figured you'd keep the books and focus on our marketing strategy.
Kayla	I'm afraid I don't know a lot about advertising.
Mary	That's okay, we can figure that part out together. We can always hire an outside agency to help us with advertising.
Kayla	I have an idea, we can give out samples and business cards in the park. That might drive customers to our business, or at least spread word of mouth.
Mary	Great! And you said you didn't know much about advertising!
Kayla	Maybe I'll do better at it than I initially thought.
Mary	So what do you think, are you in?
Kayla	I think it's a good idea and we could be successful if we work hard. Let's talk about it more next week.
Mary	Sounds like a plan!

True or False

1. Kayla is a marketing major. ········· True / False

2. Kayla has some ideas about how to bring customers to the business. ········· True / False

3. Kayla is slightly skeptical about the idea of starting a business with Mary. ········· True / False

Useful Expressions

1. I've been thinking

2. We should go into business together.

   – We have to start a business together.

3. Sounds like a plan!

READING 1

The New Clothing Store

Fill in the blanks

investment	averaging	product	expenses

A new clothing store opened up in town. At first, people were really excited about the new store. The new store had many customers and they sold a lot of ______________. For the first week, they were ______________ $500-700 in sales everyday. As the weeks went by, excitement about the store dimmed and the business started to slow. Sales dropped and they began averaging $200-300 in sales everyday. The store was not making enough money to meet their ______________. They needed to reach a new audience or to sell something new and exciting in their store. The store took a risk and hired a marketing company to promote their store. Their ______________ paid off. Soon, the store was back to averaging close to $1,000 in sales everyday.

KEY-WORDS

account: 회계, 계산, 계산서, 청구서 **successful**: 성공한, 좋은 결과의, 잘된; 번창하는
demand: 요구, 청구 **specialize**: 전문으로 하다 **unique**: 유일(무이)한, 하나밖에 없는, 독특한
strategy: 전략, 작전 **initially**: 처음에 **dim**: 어둑한, 어스레한, 애매한 **make money**: 돈을 벌다
meet one's expenses: ~지출을 감당하다 **investment**: 투자

READING 2

Starting a New Business

Starting a new business can be tough. There are many things to consider and plan for. There are start-up costs and there is a lot of work that goes into preparation. Most businesses will not see a profit for the first two years.

First, the market needs to be considered. Is now a good time to open a new business? Which location will maximize profit? Who is the target audience? Are there competitors and how will you beat them out? Answering these questions will help determine whether or not the business will be successful.

Next, consider staff and employees. All employees should be compensated fairly and should be provided with a benefits package. Think about how this will cut into any profits made by the business. How many employees will the business require? Aside from running the business, the business will require someone to handle finances, marketing, and supply.

Additionally, real estate, and taxes are something to think about. A new business requires a special license from the town. Once registered, the business will be taxed at the end of each year. On top of that, the real estate purchased (or rented) for the business will be taxed. The money the business makes over the year hopefully outweighs the start up and maintenance costs.

When thinking of starting a new business, it's wise to consult a lawyer and a financial consultant. Talk with a business consultant as well, of course!

COMPREHENSION

1. What are some things to consider before starting a business?

2. Who should you consult before starting a business?

3. What money does a business have to spend?

4. What do you think the chances are of a new business being successful? Why?

SUMMARY DISCUSSION QUESTIONS

1. Have you ever considered opening a business? What kind?

2. What are the pros and cons of opening a business?

3. How can a business be successful?

4. What are some factors that can cause a business to fail?

Grammar+

That sounds interesting.

재밌겠다. / 흥미롭다. (흥미롭게 들린다.)

감각동사+형용사

– look, sound, smell, taste, feel+형용사
~하게 보이다 / 들리다 / 냄새가 나다 / 맛이 나다 / 느낌이 나다

KEY-WORDS

consider: 숙고하다, 두루 생각하다, 고찰하다; 검토하다 **preparation**: 준비; 예비 조사, 예습 (시간) **beat out**: 따라잡다, 물리치다 **whether or not**: 어떻게 됐든, 아무튼, 하여간 **compensate**: 보상하다 **real estate**: 부동산

EXTRA UNIT

Grammar Improvement

Grammar Point 1. 분사와 분사구문

Grammar Point 2. 과거와 현재완료

Grammar Point 3. 관계사

Grammar Point 4. 수동태

Grammar Point 5. to부정사

Grammar Point 1. 분사와 분사구문

❶ 분사

분사는 형용사처럼 쓰여 명사를 수식하거나 주어나 목적어를 보충 설명하는 보어 역할을 한다.

1) 현재분사 (v-ing)

'~하는' (능동) , '~하고 있는'(진행)의 의미를 가진다.

shocking news / a sleeping baby
놀라운 뉴스 / 잠을 자고 있는 아기

- It was a shocking news.
  그것은 놀라운 뉴스였어.

- Look at the sleeping baby. She is so cute.
  자고 있는 아기를 좀 봐. 그녀는 정말 귀여워.

2) 과거분사(-ed)

'~된 (수동), '~한'(완료)의 의미를 가진다.

shocked people / a broken mirror
놀란 사람들 / 깨진 거울

- After the accident, I could see the shocked people.
  그 사건 후에 나는 놀란 사람들을 볼 수 있었다.

- I found the broken mirror under your bed. Did you break it?
  나는 그 깨진 거울을 니 침대 밑에서 찾았어. 네가 깼니?

⊙ A-B-C 형 (원형, 과거형, 과거분사형이 모두 다른 동사)

원형	과거	과거분사	의미
be	was, were	been	~이다
begin	began	begun	시작하다
break	broke	broken	부서지다
do	did	done	하다
draw	drew	drawn	그리다
drink	drank	drunk	마시다
drive	drove	driven	운전하다
eat	ate	eaten	먹다
fall	fell	fallen	떨어지다
fly	flew	flown	날다
give	gave	given	주다
get	got	got, gotten	얻다

원형	과거	과거분사	의미
go	went	gone	가다
grow	grew	grown	성장하다
know	knew	known	알다
ride	rode	ridden	타다
see	saw	seen	보다
sing	sang	sung	노래하다
speak	spoke	spoken	말하다
swim	swam	swum	수영하다
take	took	taken	가지고 가다 획득하다
wake	woke	waken	일어나다
wear	wore	worn	입다
write	wrote	written	쓰다

⊙ A-B-B 형 (과거형과 과거분사형이 같은 동사)

원형	과거	과거분사	의미
bring	brought	brought	데려오다, 가져오다
build	built	built	짓다, 세우다
buy	bought	bought	사다
catch	caught	caught	잡다
feel	felt	felt	느끼다
find	found	found	찾다
have	had	had	가지다
hear	heard	heard	듣다
lead	led	led	이끌다
leave	left	left	떠나다
keep	kept	kept	유지하다
make	made	made	만들다
lose	lost	lost	잃어버리다

원형	과거	과거분사	의미
meet	met	met	만나다
say	said	said	말하다
sit	sat	sat	앉다
sleep	slept	slept	자다
spend	spent	spent	써버리다
stand	stood	stood	서다
teach	taught	taught	가르치다
tell	told	told	말하다
think	thought	thought	생각하다
understand	understood	understood	이해하다
win	won	won	이기다
pay	paid	paid	지불하다
sell	sold	sold	팔다

◉ A-A-A 형 (원형, 과거형, 과거분사형이 모두 같은 동사)

원형	과거	과거분사	의미	원형	과거	과거분사	의미
cut	cut	cut	자르다	put	put	put	넣다, 두다
hit	hit	hit	치다	set	set	set	차리다
let	let	let	…하게 하다	spread	spread	spread	펼치다
cost	cost	cost	가격이 …이다	read[rid]	read[red]	read[red]	읽다

◉ A-B-A 형 (원형과 과거분사형이 같은 동사)

원형	과거	과거분사	의미	원형	과거	과거분사	의미
become	became	become	…이 되다	run	ran	run	달리다
come	came	come	오다				

명사를 수식하는 분사

The **sleeping** baby is my son. (명사 수식)

그 자고있는 아기는 나의 아들이다.

He has a book **written** in Korean. (명사 수식)

그는 한국어로 쓰여진 책을 가지고 있다.

주어나 목적어를 보충설명하는 분사

Ruby walked singing a song.(주격 보어)

Ruby는 노래를 부르며 걸었다.

He heard his name called. (목적격 보어)

그는 그의 이름이 불리는 것을 들었다.

exciting(흥분되게 하는)	– excited(흥분한)
surprising(놀라게 하는)	– surprised(놀란)
amazing(놀라운)	– amazed(놀란)
shocking(충격적인)	– shocked(충격 받은)
boring(지루한)	– bored(지루해하는)
tiring(피곤하게 하는)	– tired (피곤한)

The comic book was boring.
그 만화책은 지루하다.

I am bored. Do you have some books to read?
나 지루해. 읽을 책 좀 있어?

+) 현재분사와 동명사의 구분

- 현재분사: She is teaching English. (she ≠ teaching English)
  그녀는 영어를 가르치고 있다.

- 동명사: My job is teaching English. (My job = teaching English)
  나의 직업은 영어를 가르치는 것이다.

- 현재분사+명사
  a sleeping baby (a baby who is sleeping)
  잠을 자고 있는 아기

- 동명사+명사
  a sleeping bag (a bag for sleeping)
  잠을 자기 위한 가방

❷ 분사구문

부사절(접속사+주어+동사)을 현재분사(v-ing) 형태로 줄여 쓴 구문을 분사 구문이라고 한다.

1) 분사구문 형태

종속절의 주어가 주절의 주어와 같을 때, 종속절의 접속사와 주어를 생략하고 동사를 v-ing 형태로 바꾼다.

+) 종속절: 종속이란 어딘가에 속해 있다는 의미를 가지고 있으며 영어 문장에서 종속절은 접속사가 이끄는 문장을 말한다.
주절: 말 그대로 주인 문장이다.

eg. When I was young, I liked to play with my brother.
종속절 / 주절

= I liked to play with my bother when I was young.

[종속절(접속사가 이끄는 문장)이 주절보다 앞서는 경우에는 ','를 쓴다]

When **he** saw her, **he** ran away. (종속절과 주절의 주어가 같음)
그가 그녀를 보았을 때 그는 도망가버렸다.

⬇

~~When he~~ saw her, he ran away. (접속사와 주어를 생략)

⬇

Seeing her, he ran away. (동사를 원형으로 바꾸고 v-ing 형태로 쓴다.)

When I was walking down the street, I heard a strange sound.

내가 거리를 걷고 있을 때, 나는 이상한 소리를 들었다.

↓

Being walking down the street, I heard strange sound.

↓

~~Being~~ walking down the street, I heard strange sound.

↓

Walking down the street, I heard strange sound.

동사가 진행형인 경우 **being을 생략하고 v-ing**만 남긴다.

2) 분사구문의 의미

1. 시간, 때: ~할 때(when), ~하는 동안(while)

Watching TV, she fell asleep.

그녀는 TV를 보는 동안 잠이 들어버렸다.

= While she was watching TV, she fell asleep.

2. 동시동작: ~하면서

Listening to music, I studied math.

나는 음악을 들으면서 수학을 공부했다.

= As I listened to music, I studied math.

3. 이유, 원인: ~ 때문에(as, because,since)

Feeling tired, I went home early.

나는 피곤해서 집에 일찍 갔다.

= Because I felt tired, I went home early.

4. 조건 :~ 한다면(if)

Taking this bus, You can go to Odong-do.

이 버스를 타면 당신은 오동도에 갈 수 있어요.

= If you take this bus you can go to Odong-do.

5. 양보: ~에도 불구하고(though, although)

Though being sick, I went to work.

나는 아팠음에도 불구하고 일하러 갔다.

= Though I was sick, I went to work.

* 분사구문이 나타내는 뜻을 분명하게 하기 위해서 접속사를 생략하지 않고 그대로 두는 경우도 있다.

conversation

A Excuse me, Can you show me how to get to Odong-do?

실례합니다. 오동도 어떻게 가는지 알려주실 수 있나요?

B Sure. Can you see a bus stop over there?

물론이죠. 저기에 버스정류장 보이세요?

A You mean the blue sign next to the payphone?

공중전화 옆에 파란 표지판 말인가요?

B Yes. There is only one bus which stops at the bus stop.

Taking the bus, you can go to Odong-do.

네, 저 버스정류장에 서는 버스가 하나 있어요.

그 버스를 타시면 오동도에 갈 수 있습니다.

A Thanks!

감사합니다.

B No worries.

괜찮아요.

Check up

다음 문장을 분사구문으로 바꾸시오.

1. When I was young, I liked to play with my brother.

내가 어렸을 때, 나는 내 남동생과 함께 노는 것을 좋아했다.

____

2. Because I felt tired, I went home early.

피곤해서 나는 일찍 귀가했다.

____

3. If you take this bus you can go to Odong-do.

이 버스를 타면 당신은 오동도에 갈 수 있어요.

____

4. While she was watching TV, she fell asleep.

그녀가 TV를 보는 동안 그녀는 잠이 들었다.

____

5. As I listened to music, I studied math.

나는 음악을 들으면서 수학을 공부했다.

____

Grammar Point 2. 과거와 현재완료

① 과거와 현재완료

1) 과거

현재와는 상관없이 과거에 일어난 사실만을 나타낼 때 쓴다.

- I lost my car key yesterday.
  나는 어제 내 차 열쇠를 잃어버렸다. (현재 찾았는지 알 수 없다.)

2) 현재완료

과거의 한 시점에서 일어난 일이 현재까지 영향을 줄 때 쓴다.

- I have lost my car key.
  나는 내 차 열쇠를 잃어버렸다.
  (그래서 현재 차 열쇠를 가지고 있지 않다.)

② 현재완료의 형태와 뜻

주어+have(has)+과거분사

1) 완료

'막 ~했다'의 의미로 어떤 동작이 현재에 막 완료되었음을 나타냄.
주로 **already, just, yet** 등과 함께 쓰임

- I have just finished dinner.
  나 이제 막 저녁식사를 마쳤어.

- Emma has already arrived here.
  Emma는 이미 여기 도착했다.

* already, just, yet은 꼭 현재완료 형태가 아니더라도 과거형에서 쓰이기도 한다.

2) 경험

'~한 적이 있다'는 의미로 현재까지의 경험을 나타내며 주로 ever, never, before, once 등과 쓰인다.

- I have never eaten Thai food.
  나는 태국음식을 전혀 먹어본 적이 없다.

- Nate has been to Spain once.
  Nate는 스페인에 한 번 가보았다.

3) 계속

'지금까지 계속 ~해 왔다'의 의미로 과거의 어느 시점부터 지금까지 어떤 동작이나 사건이 계속되고 있음을 나타내나. 주로 since, for 등으로 쓰인다.

- I have known her for 15years.
  나는 그녀를 15년 동안 알고 있다.

- He has had dogs since he was young.
  그는 어릴 때부터 개들을 가지고 있다.

since+시점: ~이래로 for+기간: ~동안 (숫자를 포함한 구체적인 기간)

4) 결과

'~해버렸다'의 이미로 과거 행동으로 인한 결과가 현재까지 영향을 미치고 있음을 나타낸다.

- Judy has gone to London. (So she is not here now.)
  Judy는 런던으로 갔다. (그래서 지금 그녀는 여기에 없다.)

- I have lost my books. (So I don't have books now.)
  나는 나의 책들을 잃어버렸다. (그래서 나는 지금 책들을 가지고 있지 않다.)

+) have(has) gone은 가버리고 지금 여기에 없다는 의미로 결과를 나타내고
have(has) been은 가본 적이 있다는 의미로 경험을 나타낸다.

conversation

A Have you been to Austria, Jack?
Jack, 너 오스트리아에 가본 적 있어?

B Yes, I studied in Austria 5 years ago.
응, 나 5년 전에 오스트리아에서 공부했어.

A Oh, What did you study?
오, 뭐 공부했어?

B Music, of course.
음악이지 당연히.

A Then, have you seen the kangaroos and the Koalas?
그럼 캥거루들이랑 코알라들도 본 적 있어?

B Hey, Karl. They live in AUSTRALIA, dude.
야, Karl. 그것들은 오스트레일리아에 살아, 친구야.

Check up

다음 우리말을 영어로 옮기시오.

1. 나는 일본에 가 본적이 없다.

____

2. 그녀는 어제 지갑을 잃어버렸다.

____

3. 그는 시계를 잃어버렸다. (그는 시계를 지금 가지고 있지 않다.)

____

4. 그녀와 나는 2003년도부터 알고 지냈다.

____

5. Kyeonghwa는 3일 동안 아팠다.

____

6. 내 상사는 미국에 갔다. (그래서 지금 없다.)

____

7. 나는 어젯밤에 Tom을 만났다.

____

Grammar Point 3. 관계사

① 관계대명사

접속사와 대명사 역할을 하며, 관계대명사가 이끄는 절은 선행사(앞 문장의 명사)를 수식하며 선행사 바로 뒤에 쓴다.

eg. I have a friend. + She sings well.

I have a friend who sings well. [who sings well이 a friend를 수식함]

나는 노래를 잘하는 친구가 있다.

선행사	주격	목적격	소유격
사람	who	who(whom)	whose
사물, 동물	which	which	whose

1) 주격 관계대명사 who, which

관계대명사가 주어 대신에 대신 쓰임

Sue is the girl. + She lives next door. (선행사가 사람)

Sue는 그 소녀이다. 그녀는 옆집에 산다.

⬇

Sue is the girl who lives next door.

Sue는 옆집에 사는 소녀이다.

I found a cafe. + The cafe has great coffee.(선행사가 사물)

나는 한 카페를 찾았다. 그 카페는 맛있는 커피를 가지고 있다.

⬇

I found a cafe which has great coffee.

나는 커피가 맛있는 카페를 찾았다.

(나는 훌륭한 커피를 가지고 있는 카페를 찾았다.)

2) 목적격 관계대명사 who(m), which

관계대명사가 목적어 대신에 쓰이며 **생략이 가능**하다.

Katie is my friend. +I can trust her.

Katie는 내 친구이다. 나는 그녀를 믿을 수 있다.

⬇

Katie is my friend who(m) I can trust.

(=Katie is my friend I can trust.)

Katie는 내가 믿을 수 있는 친구이다.

The movie was strange. +We watched it last night.

그 영화는 이상했다. 우리는 그것을 지난 밤에 봤다.

⬇

The movie which we watched last night was strange.

(= The movie we watched last night was strange.)

지난 밤에 우리가 본 그 영화는 이상했다.

+) 목적격 관계대명사는 생략이 가능한 반면, 주격 관계대명사는 혼자서 절대 생략할 수 없지만 **[주격 관계대명사+be동사]의 형태인 경우 생략**이 가능하다.

I know the girl who lives next door.

~~I know the girl lives next door.~~

I know the girl who is singing on the stage.

⬇

I know the girl singing on the stage.

나는 그 무대 위에서 노래하고 있는 그 소녀를 알아.

3) 소유격 관계대명사 whose

소유격이므로 명사가 뒤따른다.

I like the girl. + Her eyes are blue. (선행사가 사람)

나는 그 소녀를 좋아해. 그녀의 눈은 파란색이야.

↓

I like the girl whose eyes are blue.

나는 눈이 파란 그 소녀를 좋아한다.

I want to buy the house. + Its roof is red. (선행사가 사물)

나는 그 집을 사고싶어. 그것의 지붕은 빨간색이야.

↓

I want to buy the house which roof is red.

나는 지붕이 빨간 그 집을 사고 싶다.

4) 관계대명사 that

선행사의 종류와 상관없이 주격, 목적격 관계대명사로 쓸 수 있다.

(who(m), which처럼 목적격 대명사로 쓰이거나, 주격 대명사로 쓰여 be동사와 함께 생략이 가능하다.)

Sue is the girl who lives next door.

= Sue is the girl that lives next door.

Sue는 옆 집에 사는 그 소녀이다.

The movie which we watched last night was strange.

= The movie that we watched last night was strange.

지난 밤에 우리가 본 그 영화는 이상했다.

+) 관계대명사 who(m)이나 which가 아닌 that을 써야 하는 경우

⦿ 선행사가 사람과 사물[동물]일 때

The movie is about an old man and a dog **that** lived in Japan.

그 영화는 일본에 사는 한 늙은 남자와 개에 관한 것이다.

⦿ 최상급(the -est), 서수(the first..), the very, the same, the last 등의 수식을 받는 경우

Tom was the last person that left the stage.

Tom이 무대를 떠난 마지막 사람이었다.

⦿ -thing 으로 끝나는 단어를 포함하는 경우

Do anything that you want.

니가 원하는 아무거나 해.

+) that을 쓸 수 없는 경우

관계대명사 앞에 전치사가 있을 때는 that을 쓰거나 생략할 수 없다.

다음 문장처럼 관계대명사가 전치사의 목적어인 경우 전치사를 그대로 두며 전치사는 관계대명사 앞으로 옮겨 쓸 수 있다.

I want to buy a house **which** I live **in**.

나는 내가 살 집을 하나 사고싶다.

⬇

I want to buy a house **in which** I live.

~~I want to buy a house in that I live.~~

5) 관계대명사 what

what은 선행사를 포함하고 있는 관계대명사로 the thing(s) that과 같은 의미이다.

The thing that I need now is time.

⬇

What I need now is time.

내가 지금 필요한 것은 시간이다.

② 관계부사

> 접속사와 부사의 역할(시간, 장소, 이유, 방법)을 하며, 관계부사가 이끄는 절이 형용사처럼 선행사를 수식한다.

Tell me the time. +you arrive at the airport at the time.

그 시간을 나에게 말해. 너는 그 시간에 공항에 도착한다.

↓

Tell me **the time** when you arrive at the airport.

when you arrive at thee airport가 the time을 수식

네가 공항에 도착하는 시간을 말해 줘.

* 앞서 배운 관계대명사에서 관계대명사가 전치사의 목적어인 경우 전치사를 생략하지 않고 관계대명사 앞으로 옮겨 썼던 것을 잘 기억한다.

1) when: 시간

선행사가 the time, the day, the year 등

I remember the day. +I first saw my boy friend on that day.

나는 그 날을 기억한다. 나는 내 남자친구를 그 날 처음 봤다.

↓

I remember the day which I first saw my boy friend on.

↓

I remember the day on which I first saw my boy friend.

↓

I remember the day when I first saw my boy friend.

나는 내가 내 남자친구를 처음 봤던 날을 기억한다.

2) where: 장소

선행사가 the place, the city, the country 등

I'm looking for a hotel. +I will stay at the hotel in Italy.

나는 호텔을 찾고 있다. 나는 이탈리아에서 그 호텔에서 묵을 것이다.

⬇

I'm looking for a hotel which I will stay at in Italy.

⬇

I'm looking for a hotel at which I will stay in Italy.

⬇

I'm looking for a hotel where I will stay in Italy.

나는 이탈리아에서 묵을 호텔을 찾고 있다.

3) why: 이유

선행사가 the reason

I can't say the reason. +I love him for that reason.

나는 그 이유를 말할 수 없어. 나는 그를 그 이유로 사랑해.

⬇

I can't say the reason which I love him for.

⬇

I can't say the reason for which I love him.

⬇

I can't say the reason why I love him.

나는 내가 그를 사랑하는 이유를 말할 수 없어.

how: 방법

선행사가 the way

* 선행사 the way와 관계부사 how는 함께 쓰지 않고 둘 중 하나만 쓴다.

This is the way. + I solved the problem in this way.

이것이 그 방법이다. 나는 그 문제를 이 방법으로 풀었다.

↓

This is the way which I solved the problem in.

↓

This is the way in which I solved the problem.

↓

~~This is the way how I solved the problem.~~

This is the way I solved the problem.

or

This is how I solved the problem.

이것이 내가 그 문제를 푼 방법이다.

conversation

A Do you remember the day when we first met?

당신은 우리가 처음 만났던 날을 기억해요?

B Absolutley, I remember the day.

당연히 그렇고 말고.

A I would like to visit the bar where we drank the cocktail.

우리가 칵테일을 마셨던 그 바에 가고 싶네요.

B Shall we go there this Friday?

이번 금요일에 갈까요?

A That's what I wanted to say. I'd love to! I love you.

내가 말하고 싶었던 거예요. 정말 좋아요! 사랑해요.

B I love you, too.

나도 사랑해.

Check up

다음 문장을 관계사를 이용하여 한 문장으로 쓰시오.

1. I have a friend. +She sings well.

____

2. I found a cafe. +The cafe has great coffee.

____

3. Katie is my friend. +I can trust her.

____

4. I like the girl. +Her eyes are blue.

____

5. Tell me the time. +you arrrivee at the airport at the time.

____

6. I remember the day. +I first saw my boy friend on that day.

____

7. I'm looking for a hotel. +I will stay at the hotel in Italy.

____

8. I can't say the reason. +I love him for that reason.

____

9. This is the way. +I solve the problem in this way.

____

Grammar Point 4. 수동태

+) 능동태

주어가 어떤 동작을 하는 것을 말할 때 쓴다.

Many people love the singer. 〈능동태〉

많은 사람들이 그 가수를 사랑한다.

+) 수동태

주어가 동사의 영향을 받거나 동작을 당하는 것을 말할 때 사용한다.

수동태는 공문서나 편지 등 정중하고 격식을 차리는 글에 많이 사용되므로 익숙해지는 것이 좋다.

형태 :be+과거분사

The singer is loved by many people. 〈수동태〉

그 가수는 많은 사람들에 의해서 사랑받는다.

능동태의 목적어가 주어가 되고 주어는 보통 by 뒤에서 행위자가 된다.

1 [by + 행위자]의 생략

행위자가 막연한 일반인인 경우나, 분명하지 않거나 문장의 내용상 중요하지 않을 때 [by+행위자]를 생략할 수 있다.

- English is spoken in many countries.
  영어는 많은 나라들에서 말해진다.

- The building was built in 1885.
  그 건물은 1885년에 지어졌다.

- Many people were killed in the war.
  많은 사람들이 전쟁에서 죽임을 당했다.

❷ 수동태의 시제

1) 과거시제

be동사의 과거형+과거분사

Jeonghyeon took this picture.

정현이가 이 사진을 찍었다.

↓

This picture was taken by Jeonghyeon.

이 사진은 정현이에 의해서 찍혔다.

2) 미래시제

will be+과거분사

I will write the letter.

나는 그 편지를 쓸거야.

↓

The letter will be written by me.

그 편지는 나에 의해 씌여질거야.

3) 진행시제

be동사+being+과거분사

Suhyeon is cooking dinner.

수현이는 저녁식사를 요리하고 있다.

↓

Dinner is being cooked by Suhyeon.

저녁식사가 수현에 의해서 요리되고 있다.

3 수동태의 여러 가지 형태

1) 수동태의 부정문

be 동사가 있는 문장이므로 be동사+not+과거분사

The wall was not (wasn't) painted by my dad.
그 벽은 우리 아빠에 의해 칠해지지 않았다.

2) 수동태의 의문문

수동태의 부정문과 마찬가지로 be 동사가 있는 문장이므로 be동사와 주어의 위치가 바뀐다. be동사+주어+과거분사?

Were you bitten by a bug?
너는 벌레에 물렸니?

3) 조동사의 수동태

조동사+be+과거분사 (조동사 다음에 오는 동사는 동사 원형이므로)

Your order will be shipped tomorrow.
당신의 주문은 내일 배송될 것입니다.

4) 동사구의 수동태

동사구는 수동태로 바꿀 때 하나의 동사로 취급한다.

⊙ 여러 가지 동사구

take care of	~를 돌보다	look after	~를 돌보다
run over	(차가) ~을 치다	laugh at	~를 비웃다
look up to	~을 존경하다	look down on	~을 경멸하다
bring up	~을 키우다	put off	~을 연기하다(postpone)

The babysitter took care of my sister last night.

어젯밤에 그 베이비시터가 내 여동생을 돌봤다.

↓

My sister was taken care of by the babysitter last night.

어젯밤 내 여동생은 그 베이비시터에 의해서 돌봐졌다.

The car ran over Jason.

그 차는 Jason을 쳤다.

↓

Jason was run over by the car.

Jason은 그 차에 의해서 치었다.

5) 수동태로 쓰이지 않는 동사

목적어가 없는 자동사

appear (나타나다), disappear(사라지다), happen(일어나다 / 생기다) 등

My wallet disappeared.

내 지갑이 사라졌다.

~~My wallet was disappeared.~~

소유나 상태를 나타내는 타동사

have(~을 가지고 있다), fit(~에 잘 어울리다), resemble(~을 닮다) 등

I have a car.

~~A car is had by me.~~

I resemble my dad.

~~My dad is resembled by me.~~

6) by 이외의 전치사를 사용하는 경우

보통 행위자는 by를 사용하여 나타내지만, 다른 전치사를 사용하기도 한다.

be covered with	~로 덮여 있다
be pleased with	~로 기뻐하다
be satisfied with	~에 만족하다
be disappointed with	~에 실망하다
be surprised at	~에 놀라다

be interested in	~에 흥미가 있다
be filled with (= be full of)	~로 가득차다
be known to	~에게 알려지다
be made of[from]	~로 만들어지다

I was disappointed with your mistake.

나는 너의 실수에 실망했어.

We were surprised at the news.

우리는 그 소식에 놀랐다.

conversation

A Was this table made by your husband?

이 탁자는 네 남편이 만들었어?

(이 탁자는 네 남편에 의해 만들어졌니?)

B Yes. He did it last weekend.

응. 그가 지난주에 한거야.

A He did really good job.

와, 그는 정말 잘했다.

B These chairs were made by him, too.

이 의자들도 그가 만든거야.

(이 의자들도 그에 의해서 만들어진거야.)

A Oh, my lord. he is really talented!

세상에, 그는 정말 재능이 있구나!

Check up

다음 능동태 문장을 수동태로 바꾸시오.

1. Many people love the singer.

____

2. Jeonghyeon took this picture.

____

3. I will write the letter.

____

4. Suhyeon is cooking dinner.

____

5. The babysitter took care of my sister last night.

____

6. Muse wrote this book.

____

7. He painted the wall.

____

8. The man was fixing the cmputer.

____

Grammar Point 5. to부정사

to부정사는 [to+동사원형] 형태로 문장에서 명사, 형용사, 부사의 역할을 한다. to부정사에서 부정사의 의미는 '~이 아니다'가 아니라 정해지지 않았다는 의미를 가진다. 모든 일반동사에 to를 붙여 to부정사를 만들어낼 수 있기 때문에 to부정사라고 부른다.

❶ 명사적 용법

동사로 태어났지만 to를 가짐으로써 명사(구)가 되어 문장안에서 명사의 역할을 할 수 있다.
(명사의 역할 - 주어, 목적어, 보어)

eat - to eat (먹다 - 먹는 것)

read - to read (읽다 - 읽는 것)

stop - to stop (멈추다, 그만두다 - 멈추는 것, 그만두는 것)

1) to부정사의 주어 역할

To eat breakfast is good for your health.

아침식사를 먹는 것은 너의 건강에 좋다.

= It is good for your health to eat breakfast.

* to부정사가 주어로 쓰여 길어질 경우 보통 가주어 it을 쓰고 to부정사구는 뒤로 보낸다. [it(가주어) ~ to-v(진주어)

2) to부정사의 보어 역할

My plan is to finish the project by 7:00.

나의 계획은 7시까지 그 프로젝트를 끝내는 것이다 (My paln = to finish the project)

3) to부정사의 목적어 역할

He decided to quit his job. He wants to be a teacher.

그는 그의 직업을 그만두는 것을 결심했다. 그는 선생님이 되는 것을 원한다.

◉ to부정사의 부정형 - not(never) to-v

He decided not to quit his job.

그는 그의 직업을 그만두지 않는 것을 결심했다.

4) 의문사+to-v (= 의문사+주어+should+동사원형)

문장에서 주어 목적어 보어 역할을 하며 의문사에 따라 의미가 달라진다.

what to-v: 무엇을 ~ 할지

how to-v: 어떻게 ~할지

who to-v: 누구를 ~할지

where to-v: 언제 ~할지

when to-v: 어디서(어디로) ~할지

- I don't know what to do.
  = I don't know what I should do.
  나는 무엇을 할지 모르겠어.

- Can you tell me where to go?
  = Can tou tell me where I should go?
  나에게 어디로 갈지 말해줄래요?

2 형용사적 용법

to부정사(구)가 형용사처럼 명사를 수식하기도 한다.

명사 수식

'~ 할'이라는 의미로 명사를 수식한다.

I have cold water to drink.

나는 마실 차가운 물을 가지고 있다.

* -thing, -one, - body 등으로 끝나는 명사가 올 경우 형용사의 위치가 바뀌므로 주의하고 to부정사는 형용사 뒤에 온다.

~~I have cold something to drink.~~

I have something cold to drink.

* 수식을 받는 명사가 전치사의 목적어일 때 전치사는 반드시 쓴다.

He will buy a house to live in. (live in the house)

그는 살 집을 살 것이다.

그가 안에서(in) 살 집이지 '집이 산다'는 의미가 아니다.

~~He will buy a house to live.~~

❸ 부사적 용법

to부정사(구)가 부사처럼 동사, 형용사 등을 꾸며주며, 목적, 감정의 원인 등을 나타낸다.

1) 목적

~하기 위해서 in order to(so as to)

I studied very hard to pass the exam.

= I studied very hard in order to(so as to) pass the exam.

나는 시험에 통과하기 위해서 열심히 공부했다.

2) 감정의 원인

~해서, ~하여

I was happy to see you again.

나는 당신을 다시 봐서 행복했어요.

3) 형용사 수식

~하기에

The movie is difficult to understand.

그 영화는 이해하기에 어려워.

4) 판단의 근거

~하다니

Ryan must be rude to say so.

그렇게 이야기하다니 Ryan은 무례함에 틀림없어.

5) 결과

그래서 ~하다, 하지만 결국 ~하다

He grew up to be a teacher.

그는 자라서 선생님이 되었다.

I ran fast, only to be late.

나는 빨리 달렸지만 결국 늦었다.

6) 조건

~라면, ~한다면

To hear him sing, you would believe he is a singer.

그가 노래하는 것을 듣는다면 너는 그가 가수라는 것을 믿을 거야.

4 too + 형용사 + to + 동사원형

too는 지나치게, 너무 라는 의미를 가진 부사로 부정적인 의미로만 쓰인다.

The table is too heavy to carry.

그 탁자는 너무 무거워서 나를 수가 없어.

(그 탁자는 나르기에 너무 무겁다.)

The chair is too small to sit on.

그 의자는 너무 작아서 앉을 수가 없다.

(그 의자는 앉기에 너무 작다.)

too to 용법은 so **형용사 / 부사 that** 구문으로 바꾸어 쓸 수 있다.

The car is too expensive for me to buy.

그 차는 너무 비싸서 나는 살 수가 없다.

↓

The car is **so** expensive **that** I can't buy it.

so와 that이 형용사나 부사 없이 붙어있는 경우는 다른 의미를 가지므로 유의한다.

so that: ~ 하기 위해서

eg. I save money so that I buy the car.

나는 그 차를 사기 위해서 돈을 모은다.

5 형용사 + enough to + 동사원형

~하기에 충분히 - 한

She is smart enough to pass the exam.

그녀는 그 시험에 합격하기에 충분히 똑똑하다.

enough to 역시 so 형용사 / 부사 that 구문으로 쓸 수 있다.

He is strong enough to lift the box.

그는 그 박스를 들기에 충분히 힘이 세다.

↓

He is so strong that he can lift the box.

conversation

Ⓐ Good morning, sir. Are you ready to check-out?

좋은 아침입니다, 손님. 체크아웃 할 준비가 되셨나요?

Ⓑ Oh, My. What time is it?

아, 이런. 몇시죠?

Ⓐ It's 11:10, sir.

11시 10분입니다, 손님.

Ⓑ I'm so sorry to be late. I'll check-out in 5minutes.

늦어서 죄송합니다. 5분 후에 체크아웃할게요.

Ⓐ No problem. Take your time.

괜찮습니다. 천천히 하세요.

Check up

1) 다음 우리말을 to부정사를 사용하여 영어로 옮기시오.

1. 책을 많이 읽는 것은 좋은 습관이다.

2. 너를 만나서 행복했어.

3. 나는 신발을 사려고 가게에 갔어.

4. 그는 마실 물이 필요해.

5. 그녀는 읽을 재미있는 무언가 필요해.

2) 다음 문장을 so 형용사 / 부사 that 구문으로 바꾸시오.

1. She is too young to watch the movie.

2. May is too weak to break the pole.

3. I am too busy to go shopping.

4. I am smart enough to solve the problem.

5. The car is cheap enough for me to buy.

본문 출처 및 참고 문헌

Unit 1. Greetings & Introductions

- Meeting for the First Time by Muse J.H.Lim
- Sports & extracurriculars in schools by Catherine Lynn Carriero

Unit 2. Offering Congratulations

- A New Job by Catherine Lynn Carriero and Muse J.H.Lim
- Getting Married by Catherine Lynn Carriero and Muse J.H.Lim

Unit 3. TV Show

- eBooks by Muse J.H.Lim
- Podcasts by Catherine Lynn Carriero

Unit 4. Eating Out

- Cooking a Simple Meal by Muse J.H.Lim
- Eating at a Fancy Restaurant by Catherine Lynn Carriero

Unit 5. Shopping

- The Mall by Catherine Lynn Carriero and Muse J.H.Lim
- Amazon: Pros & Cons by Catherine Lynn Carriero

Unit 6. At the Airport

- Airlines Saving Money by Catherine Lynn Carriero
- Tips & Tricks at the Airport by Catherine Lynn Carriero and Muse J.H.Lim

Unit 7. At a Hotel

- A New Hotel by Catherine Lynn Carriero and Muse J.H.Lim
- A Pamphlet from a Hotel in Connecticut by Catherine Lynn Carriero

Unit 8. Having a Party

- Christmas by Catherine Lynn Carriero and Muse J.H.Lim
- A Golden Anniversary by Catherine Lynn Carriero

Unit 9. Job Interview

- My Qualifications by Catherine Lynn Carriero and Muse J.H.Lim
- Remote Interviews by Catherine Lynn Carriero

Unit 10. Business

- The New Clothing Store by Catherine Lynn Carriero and Muse J.H.Lim
- Starting a New Business by Catherine Lynn Carriero

Extra Unit. Grammar Improvement

- Basic Grammar in use / Raymond Murphy with William R. Smalzer / Cambridge (2011)
- Grammar in use Intermediate / Raymond Murphy / Cambridge (2011)
- Advanced Grammar in use / Martin Hewings / Cambridge (2011)
- Grammar Inside Level 2 / 능률영어교육연구소 / 능률 (2015)

저자 약력

김경태

현) 한영대학교 호텔관광과 학과장
여수시 MICE산업 지원위원회 위원
여수 낭만투어 버스 운영 사업자 선정 심의위원
광주·전남형 스마트 관광인력 양성 사업단 위원
(사)부산관광마이스진흥회 전문위원
(사)한국식음료교육협회 정회원
전) 특급호텔 Sales & Marketing 부서 등 18년 근무

이근홍

현) 한영대학교 호텔관광과 교수
한영대학교 입학관리처장, 전자계산소장
전) 한영대학교 교학처장, 평생교육원장
여수시 정보기술교육원 원장

임정현

현) 한영대학교 외래강사
E-World Academy 회화강사
전) 충덕중학교 수준별 강사

Lyceum Education Centre, Melbourne VIC Austrailia
- Certificated IV in ESL PRofessional
Milner International College of English, Perth WA Austrailia
- Certificated TESOL Course

경희사이버대학교 한국어문화학 전공
전남대학교 영어영문학 전공

Catherine Lynn Carriero

- Present - Westchester School of Speech and Drama; Drama Teacher
- Present - The Human, Earth Project; CEO
- Four Corner Productions; Producer
- E-World Academy; Lead Teacher
- Nittany Theatre at the Barn, House Stage Manager
- The Slusarz Law Firm, LLC, Web Designer and Assistant

TESOL Certified
Pennsylvania State University; University Park Bachelor of Arts Degree

Practical College English [실용대학영어]

초판 발행 2021년 12월 30일
지은이 김경태 · 이근홍 · 임정현 · Catherine Lynn Carriero
펴낸이 김중용
총괄기획 최준규
편 집 심성보
펴낸곳 도서출판 정독
경기도 고양시 일산서구 하이파크로 113, 102-204
등록 제406-2014-000093호
전 화 070)7550-3758 팩 스 02)718-8554
홈페이지 www.jeongdok.co.kr 이메일 pnc@pncmedia.co.kr
ISBN 979-11-6858-003-9 93740

정 가 20,000원

이 교재는 2021년도 한영대학교 교양교육융합센터 혁신지원사업비로 진행되었습니다.